Printed in the United States of America. First Printing, 2020
Publisher
Williams Commerce, LLC

Visit Our Website Williamscommerce1.com ISBN 978-0-578-75488-8

“A curly hair affirmation for every day of the month.”

Written By: Janel Caminos

Affirmation 1

"My curls are
perfectly
made by
Him."

Affirmation 2

"I am proud
of my curls."

Affirmation 3

"I am proud
to wear my
curly crown
daily."

Affirmation 4

"With my curls I will arise."

Affirmation 5

"I will
accept my
curls."

Affirmation 6

"No
weapons
formed
against
my curls
and I
shall
prosper."

Affirmation 7

"Today
will be a
good hair
day."

Affirmation 8

"I will not
let anyone
dim my
curls."

Affirmation 9

"My hair is professional hair."

Affirmation 10

"I embrace
my curls."

Affirmation 11

"I love my
God given
curls."

Affirmation 12

"I will not be ashamed
of my curls."

Affirmation 13

"I will not straighten my curls to be accepted."

Affirmation 14

"My
curls
make
me
beautiful
and
unique."

Affirmation 15

“God took His time creating each curl.”

Affirmation 16

“I will rock my
pineapple.”

Affirmation 17

"Every day is a hot curly girl summer."

Affirmation 18

"There is
purpose
in my
curls."

Affirmation 19

"Today I will recognize another curlfriend."

Affirmation 20

"I
choose
to be
patient
with
myself
and my
curls."

Affirmation 21

"I choose to make
myself and my
curls a priority."

Affirmation 22

"I give my curls the love I desire to have."

Affirmation 23

"I love my curls
unconditionally."

Affirmation 24

"I refuse to settle for less than
what my curls and I deserve."

Affirmation 25

"I reject any
negative curl
talk today."

Affirmation 26

"I choose self-love and my curls."

Affirmation 27

"I am as
precious
as my
curls."

Affirmation 28

"My curls
and I
deserve
reciprocal
love."

Affirmation 29

"My curls are
healthy and
strong."

Affirmation 30

"I appreciate myself
and my curls."

Made in the USA
Columbia, SC
21 February 2021

33290617R00038